Edmund Clarence Stedmann

The Prince's Ball

Edmund Clarence Stedmann

The Prince's Ball

ISBN/EAN: 9783743355187

Manufactured in Europe, USA, Canada, Australia, Japa

Cover: Foto ©ninafisch / pixelio.de

Manufactured and distributed by brebook publishing software
(www.brebook.com)

Edmund Clarence Stedmann

The Prince's Ball

Protected by Newcastle's Pinions,
We start for Uncle Sam's Dominions.

A Brochure.

FROM "VANITY FAIR."

BY EDMUND C. STEDMAN,

Author of "The Diamond Wedding," "Lyrics and Idyls," etc.

With Illustrations by Stephens.

NEW YORK:

RUDD & CARLETON, 130 GRAND STREET,

(BROOKS BUILDING, COR. OF BROADWAY).

M DCCC LX.

E. CRAIGHEAD,

Printer, Stereotyper, and Electrotyper,

Carton Building,

81, 83 and 85 Centre Street.

CONTENTS.

——o——

THE PRINCE'S BALL.

PART I.

THE PRINCELY PROGRESS.

O, HAVEN'T you heard how an Eng-
lish Prince, prince, prince,
A genuine royal scion—
How an English Prince, not three months
since,
Came sailing, singing, dancing along,
His true American friends among?
To him I dedicate this song,
By leave of the BRITISH LION.

O, haven't you heard how an English Duke,
duke, duke—
How an English Duke his home forsook?

How, leaving his high old castle,

Newcastle came with the other two,

Prince of Wales and Lord Renfrew ?

Here are grandees three, it seems to me !

Add them up how many there be :

And while you are trying the knot to undo,

   I'll give you the rest of my parcel.

Maidens were saying, long before

He came in sight of a Yankee shore,

That all the princes of fairy rhyme,

Voyaging " once upon a time,"

Never compared with this island Prince ;

His lips were sweeter than sugared quince ;

   His locks as brown

   As Prince Charming's own ;

   When he spoke, his tone

Was nice to be heard, as that of the bird,

To which Prince Ruby was cruelly turned

By the spell his magical rival learned ;

He had just enough of the rickets in
    youth
To make him wise as Prince Ricquet, and,
    sooth,
    No tuft to make him frightful;
Prince Valiant himself was not braver;
And as to his face—I here give place
To my artist and engraver:
If they half do their duty by his beauty,
    You'll own his face is delightful.

In the morn of a warm midsummer day,
The royal party made their way
Where the ships, not far from Portsmouth
    bar,
    Lay trimmed and ready for starting;
Victoria's cheek His Highness kissed,
Heartily shook the Consort's fist,
Gave sister Alice's nose a twist,
    And so got through with the parting.

1*

Past Cape Clear and the Channel Fleet,
    Waft, breezes, waft the sweet
Young Prince, and don't be froward—
      As you are, they say,
      In the Biscay Bay;
For the jolly old Sun is shining his best
On the gold 𝔍𝔠𝔥 𝔇𝔦𝔢𝔫 of the Prince's crest,
    That flames at the HERO's peak.
" Forward ! forward ! royally toward
The loyal welcomers in the West,
    And the distant land we seek !"
But down, down, beneath the waves,
To the ocean-nymphs' and Undines' caves,
'Twas telegraphed that a mortal Prince
Was crossing the broad Atlantic waters:
So strange a thing had not happened,
    since
Prince FLOD sailed over the Northern Sea,
And was carried off by the LURLEY's daugh-
    ters;

You all have read the story, I trust;
    If you haven't, you must
    (You'll find it in THORPE's Epitome);
Then O, what a wonder the billows
    under!
For even great Neptune's Queen herself
Came up for a sight of the young GUËLPH ;*
    One by one, the Nereïd race,
Nymph and mermaid and water-fay,
To catch a glimpse of his handsome face,
Swam round the HERO every day;
Lifting themselves on their dolphin tails,
Parting their hair with fingers fair,
Peering over the vessel's rails,
Splashing, dashing, glances flashing—
Longing to capture the Prince of Wales!

* For this rhyme 'tis proper to make amends
    To some H-disdaining English friends;
    But who, without going to WALKER for—help,
    Could rhyme it at all, if pronounced Gu-elp ?

But straight for the Nova Scotian shore
    The squadron bore,
Till, after wet nights and iceberg frights,
And other usual marine delights,
    It anchored in Halifax harbor.
Here thirty thousand Jonathan Slicks,
Packed together like so many bricks,
Gave ALBERT EDWARD no time to " fix,"
    Nor the Duke to visit his barber;
Such loyalty never was known before;
Cheering, clamor, and cannons' roar,
    And still the tumult increases,
Until, by way of crowning the fun,
And showing how such things should be
    done,
    They blow a gunner to pieces.

Now how can I crowd together the tales
You all have heard, of the Prince of
    Wales

From Water-Sprites' alluring Slyness,
Newcastle saves His Royal Highness.

On his grand Canadian journey,
Without counterfeiting the newspaper-men,
Or gaining the use of a " Howard's" pen,
    By a special Power of Attorney ?
St. John's, Windsor, Quebec, and so on to
Montreal, Ottawa, Kingston, Toronto—
Parliament Houses—Victoria Bridges—
Lakes and rivers, and mountain ridges—
Cheers, addresses, riots and marches
Made, *nolens-volens*, through Orange arches;
All painted together and framed anew,
Form a very kaleidoscopic view.

My readers have heard, I take it for
    granted,
Of his going to church ; how the choristers
    chanted,
And how, when they came to the *Gloria*
    Patri,
It sounded precisely like *Gloria Matri ;*

How the Bishop went bowing him into the
 aisle,
Then preached him a sermon as long as a
 mile,
  On the duty of kings to be humble ;
While, placed in a lofty pew by himself,
On a throne of crimson, the bashful GUELPH
  Hardly dared the responses to mumble.
You have heard how he knighted NAR-
 CISSE BELLEAU,
And frightened that worthy provincial so,
That he went on both knees for the
 accolade-blow ;
How, when the Prince washed, each loyalist
 bought a
Flacon of the costly soap-and-water ;
And how a barber grew suddenly rich,
By selling each hair of the handful, which
He shingled down from the Prince's crown,
  At the very low rate of a "quarter."

And how, by a singular transformation,
While whirling across the Niagara road,
  he
Slipt out of his royal incarnation,
  And into LORD RENFREW's body.
It would give me very much pleasure to
  sing
How he speedily felt "every inch a king,"
  As one of the sovereign people;
For the first time moving among his
  mates,
Made his lightning tour of the Northern
  States,
  More quizzed than the clock on a
  steeple;
Drank lager and danced, wherever he
  chanced,
At St. Louis, Chicago, and various cities
Whose names are not suited for rhyming
  in ditties;

From his balcony bowed

Three times to each crowd;

Then escaped to the prairies, where game
were so plenty,

That, in spite of the very astonishing rent,
he

Displayed in his trousers, he shot more
than twenty;

Then, in rosewood cars and a special
train,

Whirled on to the White House, J. B., and
Miss LANE,

Where many grave things were uttered and
done,

With all sorts of etiquette-ical fun;

Then there's Richmond, and Baltimore,
Pittsburg, Porkopolis—

But what are the whole to our grander
Metropolis!

I merely name them to skip them all,

Ye Prince enjoyeth Merrilie
Ye Sweets of Reciprocitie.

And will leave ALBERT EDWARD proceed-
 ing bedward,
While I tell how the Gothamites got up
 the BALL.

PART II.

THE COUNCIL OF FOUR HUNDRED.

MEANWHILE the Lords of the Empire
    City
Were grouped together, on Church and
    'Change,
Saying—"O, what a pity! O, what a pity,
For BOOLE and his crew to be given range
    To bully, bluster, and blunder!
To go in for another such Golden Fleece
As warmed the backs of the Japanese;
Or come with their Aldermanic quids,
Marvellous grammar and yellow kids;
    To excite Lord RENFREW's wonder."

For the honor and commerce of the city,
'Twas plain to see there must be a Com
    mittee!

So men of means and might were chosen,
Score by score and dozen by dozen,
In all, four hundred noble names,
        With General Scott to lead them:
So great their fortunes and their fames,
That when the Aldermen came to read
        them,
They blessed their luminaries stellar,
And hid, abashed, in the City Hall cellar.

Thirty Presidents of banks
Were in the Committee's foremost ranks;
Half as many had banks of their own;
Nearly a score so rich had grown,
Each could start a daily paper alone;
        To give the list variety,
Plenty of lawyers were scattered through,
With judges and editors not a few,
But these of the orthodox saffron hue,
        The golden cream of society;

The Historical Rooms were represented,
And the Clubs had cause to be well con
      tented ;
Lots of the rising ticket-shares
Were held by the "UNION" millionaires,
And the "ATHENÆUM" was counted in,
Though famous rather for numbers than
      tin ;
The classic "CENTURY" furnished seven ;
Then, to give the loaf a proper leaven
Of bibliopolical taste antique,
A note was sent, in Coptic and Greek,
Requesting the "BRADFORD CLUB" to assist
In ekeing out the Committee-list ;
An answer came, in cuneiform signs ;
When read by a paleologist,
It said: "The Bradford Club declines,
      Engaged on business vital."
They were reproducing, "by special per-
      mission,"

The " Book of Genesis ; 1st Edition,
B. C. 1491."
With a steel fac-simile, fairly done,
Of MOSES' book-plate, in the title.

In fine, so stylish and wealthy a set
Were never gathered together yet—
 Full of bankers, clubmen, and scholars ;
A *Herald* reporter, who knows how to
  count,
Added up their estates to the gross amount
 Of TWO HUNDRED MILLION DOLLARS!

Birds of a feather, they came together,
 To hold a primal caucus !
It don't appear in what mystic hall
They met, or whether in daylight at all ;
 Perhaps in the shades of Orcus.
Wherever it was, the question arose—
" How do members to honor the Prince
  propose ?"

Some wanted a DINNER, and midnight
    speeches

Along with the wine and brandy-peaches;

Others on having a BALL insisted,

Which proposition the first resisted,

Till quite a dignified contest was raging;

But, while gentlemen fiercely the battle
    were waging,

One member, most potent and wealthy, be-
    gan

To speak up for the Terpsichorean plan ;

For he thought, if Lord RENFREW himself
    were to choose,

A Ball would exactly accord with his
    views:

That very accomplished and noble young
    man

Could ride, sing, and shoot, and, if need be,
    eat,

In a manner that others found hard to beat

But none of these arts
Made him Prince of Hearts,
So much as his talent for dancing;
Of all the Princes under the sun,
There surely never was such an one
For frolicking and romancing!
A dozen sets, at a frontier ball,
Hadn't begun to content him at all;
He'd dance in all sorts of weather;
His Arms should have been a fiddle and bow,
With a pair of castanets hung below,
And his plume, that charmed the young
ladies so,
(With a sala-am to Prof. INGRAHAM,)
The original Dancing Feather;
It was even said that his great delight,
Established etiquette scorning,
Would not only be to dance all night,
But —once escaped from NEWCASTLE's
sight—

To go home with the girls in the
  morning !

Then from their sofas uprose ten
Very wealthy and righteous men,
  With consciences sorely troubled :
"They'd dance if they must," but if they
  could call
The thing a Reception, instead of a Ball,"
  They'd "see their subscriptions dou-
  bled."
Four were Presbyterians blue ;
High-Church Episcopalians two ;
Low-Church Episcopalian one ;
Broad-Church Unitarian, none ;
Three were Baptists, open and close :
  All pillars in firm position.
For two, the Ball was too much of a
  dose ;
But the eight resolved, with one accord,

That, as David danced before the Lord,
They'd foot it once for the royal nonce,
Despite the risk of perdition;
Yet, the better to wash the sin away,
Each secretly vowed to shortly pay
Very much more than ever before
To the Afghanistan mission.

Thereupon the Committee voted, all,
That My Lord should have an Academy
Ball,
And the matter was settled without more
ado;
Then, as knowing rumors began to creep
through
The daily journals, of what was in view,
Very great men the Committee grew
In every one's estimation.
Little by little the news transpired,
That the grand Academy had been hired

At a fabulous computation ;
That, after this, Aladdin himself
Might lay up his rusty old lamp on the
　　shelf,
For the splendors, familiar to Genius or Elf,
Would pale by the side of those supplied
　　For Lord RENFREW's delectation.

To think how the four hundred members
　　were harassed
By thousands of friendly requests for a card !
Married and single alike were embarrassed,
(Some say they enjoyed it, but that's a
　　canard !)
Whether eating or talking, riding or walk-
　　ing,
Almost while dressing themselves and
　　undressing,
With pretty lips pouting and white arms
　　caressing,

Fair ladyes thronging, strive who can,
Cajole ye bolde Committee man.

And sweet voices wishing a maidenly bless-
    ing,
Agreeing to dance with, kiss, love, even
    wed,
Those by whom the dear girls to the Ball
    should be led!

" How many tickets for ladies ?" next
This question our members much per-
    plexed;
But a plethoric sub-committee of three
Found tailoring easy as A. B. C.,
    And took the Academy's measure;
(" If they'd fit it out with a new suit of
    clo'es,
Scenes and curtains," M. Strakosch " knows
    It would give his patrons pleasure ;")
Down on their knees they measured the
    floor,
Giving each lady five feet, and no more,

For her crinoline-diameter;
As if women advance in the mazy dance,
    In a kind of trochaic pentameter.

Those   who   havn't   read,   can   easily
        guess
Of the rules prescribed for manners and
        dress,
And what female battles began to ensue,
Betwixt Fifth and Madison Avenue,
On the delicate question, as to who
        Should dance first with the noble
        stranger;
How every young lady turned up her
        nose
At fair ones, who ventured her claims to
        oppose :
How bosom friends became mortal foes,
And jewelled fingers dealt tiny blows,
        Much fuller of spite than danger!

But who finally won the coveted honor,

And how she bore her laurels upon her—

These things, with the glory, and glitter
    and all

That was said, thought, or done at the
    PRINCE'S BALL,

Not to mingle the earthly with pleasures
    Elysian,

I reserve for my canticle's final division.

PART III.

THE ACADEMY BALL.

CLOUDS and sunshine, wind and
    rain,
And the world turns over and over
    again.
Lord Renfrew has kissed his glove to Miss
    Lane,
Whom the Gothamites have implored in
    vain
    To grace the scene of their glory;
For J. B., smoothing his cambric band,
Plainly gives them to understand
She shall follow no princes through the
    Land—
As Medea chased for Jason's hand
    In the mythologic story.

Ye Prince, in warlike guise arrayed,
Doth lead ye lengthy Cavalcade.

Passing the Quaker City's gates,
My Lord has left the United States
　　To cross the Jersey peninsula;
Has slept once more on American shore:
Ridden from Castle Garden, through
Three miles of flags—red, white, and
　　blue,
　　Walls of marble, iron, and brick—
　　Roofs and balconies, noisily thick
With thousands sprawling after a view,
'Till he's lodged on the handsomest
　　Avenue
　　Of the greatest of cities insular.

But now, as October Twelfth drew near,
What hurry and bustle, joy and fear!
Jealous hatred of those to appear,
By those whose hopes were blasted and
　　sere;
As if all the life of a hemisphere

Were mingled in hocus-pocus,
And, through Vanity's lenses flashing hot,
Made the Empire City a radiant spot,
    With Irving Place for its focus!

What costume-trying in visits flying:
Days of dress-and-jewelry buying!
A hundred mantua-makers were dying
Of sheer exhaustion, and half a score
Exchanged the smiles they usually wore
    For a reckless inurbanity;
While every tailor, from Fulton to Bond,
Declared himself in the Slough of Despond,
And solemnly swore that one order more
    Would drive him into insanity.

What scintillant splendors found display,
In mirrored windows along Broadway!
By the Vanderbilt they sent, in advance,
For jewels of Florence and silks of France.

Homeward she paddled, deeply laden,

With stuffs to made a Manhattan maiden

 A princess, minus the dowry;

To make a matron of forty years,

As fine as a Dowager Duchess appears

 In a spectacle-play, at the Bowery.

No lady-shopper could ever escape

From the robes of every fabric and shape—

Satins, taffetas, gauzes, crape;

Skirts of tulle embroidered with gold;

Watered silks in waves unrolled;

Heaviest textures, marvellous hues,

Ashes of Roses, buffs and blues;

Gros des Indies and rich brocade,

In lustrous folds and colors arrayed;

Dark Moirées, with silver garniture,

 Light Moirées, brilliant with gold and

  cherry—

Fabrics costly enough, I'm sure,

 A queen to wed, or even to bury;

Chantilly laces, Valenciennes;
Ribbons woven by Lyons men;
Fancy fans, with flower and feather,
Lavishly piled in heaps together;—
What can compare with sights so rare,
Save the Paris booth in VANITY FAIR!

There's my charming friend, Columbia V—
That lily of aristocracy!
As she sat, on the Sunday before the B.,
In her father's cushioned pew at Grace,
Did you think—when she covered her
          beautiful face,
And knelt on the crimson tabouret—
That she heard what the Doctor had to say,
Or prayed as the ritual bade her pray?
What supplications she made, have flown
Straight to the foot of fashion's throne;
The angel, who into her heart could probe,
Knew well that instead of a stainless robe,

She quite as much longed at the time to
    possess

An earthly and exquisite Renfrew dress;

That she thought to herself she would
    have it made

Of the whitest and richest striped brocade—

Striped with Magenta, and overlaid

With silken rose-buds, blossoms and
    leaves;

Low-pointed corsage and puffing sleeves

Should grace the charms of her waist and
    arms;

Over her shoulders should be set

A cape, à la Marie Antoinette,

And a bunch of myrtle and mignonette

Should bloom where the point-lace borders
    met.

Pearls and silver should intertwine

To make her a head-dress quite divine;

For her feet she will use white-satin shoes,

With mauve rosettes, encircling pearls,
So that—when in the waltz her crinoline
　　whirls,
And the tips of her toes shall catch the
　　eye
Of the Prince, he will say to the standers-by,
That she has for her feet a toilet completer
Than that of a Spanish Señorita,
And that Cinderella's could not have been
　　sweeter !

But the world turns over and over again,
With cloud and sunshine, wind and rain,
　　Love and envy and rancor.
AT LAST IT HAS COME ! the crowning night ;
The ultimatum of all delight ;
The hour, when even an anchorite
　　May be pardoned for weighing anchor,
Hoisting sails, and bearing away
To the rendezvous in Prince's Bay,

For which thousands vainly hanker;
(You see it is not the Committee's fault
That Smith or Jones isn't worth his salt
Or wasn't born a banker.)

It has come at last! How bright the
    sight
Of a Grand-Academy gala-night!
The blaze of the whirling calcium rays
Lightens the spacious entrance-ways,
Flashing on up-turned, glaring faces
Of thousands thronging about the
    squares:
Thousands, to whom your jewels and
    laces
Are things for which nobody this night
    cares.
For a sight of the Prince the people
    crowd;
To your simple hearts should be allowed

A sight of the Prince, poor people!
    since
He came to visit us one and all,
Asked or not asked to go to the Ball!
Scores of policemen will never convince
The crowd, that it oughtn't to see the
    Prince.

Up to the porch the carriages rumble,
    By yellow-plushes attended:
No wonder the laboring-men feel humble,
    In the presence of scenes so splendid!
      Never before, never before,
Such diamonds and dresses entered that
    door;
And VANITY FAIR, arrayed in its best,
    Glides in with the rest.
(It wouldn't have been so very well dres-
    sed,
If it had not carefully learned by rote

These Two will not goe in, I guesse,
Until they somewhat change their Dresse.

The words of the Secretary's note:
A compilation of information,
Which I will try to find room below to
    quote.*)

* " Without further prelude or protraction,
I have the distinguished satisfaction
To avail myself of the present chance
Of informing those invited to dance,
That no lady can enter, whose head has on it
That gross impropriety called a bonnet ;
Colonels and captains may display
The suits which they wear on training-day ;
All others must come in evening dress ;
Of course you will never be able to guess
What a gentleman wears, when *comme il faut,*
So this private note is to let you know
That legs and arms, and bosom and back,
Must be rigidly cased in cloth of black ;
White shirts and cravats, French boots for the feet,
With light-colored kids, make up the complete
Array of a member of the *élite.*
That this is authoritative to show,
I affix my name and address below. "

3

Into the radiance we glide,
As a bayou-voyager follows the tide,
From mangrove shadows and fallen trees,
To the silvery sheen of moonlit seas;
Into the glare of countless lights,
And the wedding of sweetest sounds and
      sights;
Where gilded walls and tapestried halls,
Repeat the Music's dying falls,
And flowers of multitudinous hues,
Their blended, odorous breaths diffuse.
But through the glamour we move along
To glance at the guests that with us throng,
    And study the queer variety
It takes to fashion that paradox-
Ical edifice, built on golden "rocks,"
    Entitled "Our Best Society."

Take of judges and generals, each, a pair;
Three consuls, a foreign Chargé d'Affaires:

Mayors and governors, one or two;
Of authors and scholars very few;
Congressmen, plenty as drops of dew;
Railroad presidents, bulls and bears,
Bankers, merchants, and millionaires;
These, with their daughters, sisters, and
    wives—
Three thousand wealthy and common-place
    lives —
Birds of one feather—squeeze them to-
    gether
At a Prince's Ball, and you have, in short,
An "illustrated Republican Court."

Of course, in dignity evanescent,
The famous Committee all were present;
But to neophytes, who had never been
At an Academic full-dress scene,
Grave bankers, leading off, with a will,
The gallopade of a grand quadrille,

Must have seemed, in their coats and white
  cravats,
A species of clerical acrobats,
Training, to give the Shaker profession
A numerous, Orthodox accession.
Nor would the idea be very far wrong,
For a tithe, 'tis said, to churches belong,
Whose articles hold that Dance and Song
  Are Stygian missionaries;
—Here my friend, the mathematician, says
'Tis a handy rule that works both ways,
And that condemnation with rank and
  station
  In inverse ratio varies.

Far be it from me to feel aggrieved
That the festive dance has thus received
  Official and grave endorsement;
Yet I charge these gentlemen, large and
  small,

To never again denounce a Ball,
But to stand committed, once for all,
  To what I claim their course meant.
For I never heard that the angels rate
The presence of prince or potentate,
As helping to add a pious weight
  To a carnal convocation;
And, to set the matter plain and straight,
Why should Jack be doomed to a sul-
    phurous fate,
One shudders to think of, for shaking a
    leg
And drinking his flip, with Moll and Peg,
  In the Valley of Humiliation,
While a churchly man, of plethoric purse,
Is promised treatment quite the reverse,
  For his loftier dissipation?

And what is there worse in a rustic Reel,
Merrily measured with toe and heel,

On a country-tavern's floor of deal,
While whips are cracked, and sleigh-bells
    peal
      Outside, till echo answers—
What is there worse, say my honest rhymes,
In these plain, old-fashioned, jolly good
    times,
      Where Sambo plays for the dancers,
Than in the maze of a princely show,
Where diamonds sparkle and velvets glow,
And the wave of a spruce maëstro's bow
      Beats out the time in The Lancers!

Enough, you say, of polemical rhyme;
And the ladies whisper, 'tis fully time
      For the Prince to make his appearance;
" He's coming!" " He isn't!" " Yes, that
    is he;"
And better for him, to be seen and to see,
If the flower of our aristocracy

Our countrie Friends finde Dancing pleasant,

Although no Prince of Wales be present.

Would give him a better clearance.
But as ALBERT EDWARD, young and fair,
Stood on the canopied daïs-stair,
And looked, from the circle crowding there,
To the length and breadth of the outer
    scene,
Perhaps he thought of his mother, the
    QUEEN;
(Long may her empery be serene!
Long may the heir of England prove
Loyal and tender; may he pay
No less allegiance to her love,
Than to the sceptre of her sway!)
Perhaps he wondered if this were the land,
Where Nobility's said to be based on
    Labor,
Where every man, with a strong right hand,
Can claim a title as well as his neighbor;
Perhaps he saw that we have a King,
    The potent and sovereign DOLLAR,
3*

Able the nose of the workman to bring
To the grindstone, and over his neck to fling
A heavy and feudal collar.
But what were his thoughts I can never
　　tell,
For sharply, as belle was jostling belle—
Each making a Flora-Temple " burst,"
For the honor of dancing beside him first—
The staging before him fell in with a
　　crash,
And fifty young ladies, as quick as a
　　flash,
Sank down in a kind of etherial hash,
As dainty a dish as a Prince could wish ;
　　But he passed to the supper-pavilion,
And we saw him no more, till they mended
　　the floor,
　　And opened the primal cotillion.
There, gracefully dancing with Mrs.
　　MORGAN,

Ye handsome Prince is at a losse
To whom ye Handkerchief to tosse.

He had quite forgotten his thoughts,
   I suppose,
Just as hearers a sermon forget, at its
   close,
When the "Jubilate" is played on the
   organ ;
   Whatever his fancies were, nobody
   knows.

Now, how strange the feeling that comes to
   one,
When the royal Show is almost done,
When the gas for hours has dazzled the eye,
And the air grows dense as the flowers die !
How strange to go out, from the crowded
   rout,
To the open street, where to all is given
A sight of the clear and infinite Heaven ;
Out into the cool October night,
Where, in place of that garish inner light,

Are all those silvery cressets, fed
With rays from God's own glory shed.
Ah! if one now might only flee
Across that measureless, lucid sea,
To lustres—O, how pure and far!—
What, from the spirit's chosen star,
Would all this glittering turmoil seem,
Save the fantasy of an earthly dream?

And even the Man who lives in the Moon—
(You'd reach him a million times as soon!)
Who, day after day, sees the whole round
      world
Like a map to his curious gaze unfurled—
Would perceive no increase in the polarized
      ray
      Thrown off from this part of our sphere,
Though the roof of the Opera House
      were away,
      And the lights that illumine each tier—

And all the lamps that make Paris, they
    say,
And London, as cheerful by night as by
    day,
With all in New York, together were
    burning;
To the Man in the Moon they'd be past all
    discerning;
So there's one man, at least, will know
    nothing at all
Of the splendor and fame of THE PRINCE'S
    BALL!

THE END.

NEW BOOKS

And New Editions Recently Published by

RUDD & CARLETON,

130 GRAND STREET, NEW YORK,

(BROOKS BUILDING, COR. OF BROADWAY.)

———◆———

N.B.—RUDD & CARLETON, UPON RECEIPT OF THE PRICE, WILL SEND ANY OF THE FOLLOWING BOOKS, BY MAIL, *postage free*, TO ANY PART OF THE UNITED STATES. THIS CONVENIENT AND VERY SAFE MODE MAY BE ADOPTED WHEN THE NEIGHBORING BOOKSELLERS ARE NOT SUPPLIED WITH THE DESIRED WORK.

——— ◆ ———

NOTHING TO WEAR.

A Satirical Poem. By WILLIAM ALLEN BUTLER. Profusely and elegantly embellished with fine illustrations on tinted paper, by Hoppin. Muslin, price 50 cents.

THE KELLYS AND THE O'KELLYS.

A New Novel, from the pen of ANTHONY TROLLOPE, Author of "Doctor Thorne," &c. Reprinted from the English edition. One vol., 12mo., muslin, price $1 25.

ALEXANDER VON HUMBOLDT.

A new and popular Biography of this celebrated *Savant*, including his travels and labors, with an introduction by BAYARD TAYLOR. One vol., steel portrait, price $1 25.

HUMBOLDT'S PRIVATE LETTERS.

The Correspondence of Alexander Von Humboldt with Varnhagen Von Ense, and other contemporary celebrities. From the German. Muslin, price $1 25.

CESAR BIROTTEAU.

A Novel, by HONORE DE BALZAC. The first of a Series of Translations from standard Works of this celebrated French novelist. One vol., 12mo., muslin, price $1 00.

ADVENTURES OF VERDANT GREEN.

By CUTHBERT BEDE, B.A. The best humorous story of College Life ever published. *80th edition*, from English plates. Nearly 200 original illustrations, price $1 00.

LIFE OF HUGH MILLER.

Author of "Schools and Schoolmasters," "Old Red Sandstone," &c. Reprinted from the Edinburgh edition. One large 12mo., muslin, new edition, price $1 25.

LOVE (L'AMOUR).

By M. JULES MICHELET. Author of "A History of France," &c. Translated from the French by J. W. Palmer, M.D. One vol., 12mo., muslin, price $1 00.

WOMAN (LA FEMME).

A sequel and companion to "Love" (L'Amour) by the same author, MICHELET. Translated from the French by Dr. J. W. Palmer. 12mo. Muslin, price $1 00.

DOCTOR ANTONIO.

A Love Tale of Italy. By RUFFINI, author of "Lorenzo Benoni," "Dear Experience," &c. Reprinted from the London copy. Muslin, new edition, price $1 25.

DEAR EXPERIENCE.

A Tale. By G. RUFFINI, author of "Doctor Antonio," "Lorenzo Benoni," &c. With illustrations by Leech, of the *London Punch*. 12mo., muslin, price $1 00.

THE GREAT TRIBULATION ;

Or Things coming on the Earth. By Rev. John Cumming, D.D., author of "Apocalyptic Sketches," &c. From the English edition. First Series. Muslin, price $1 00.

THE GREAT TRIBULATION.

Second Series of the new work by Rev. Dr. Cumming, which has awakened such an excitement throughout the religious community. 12mo., muslin, price $1 00.

BOOK OF THE CHESS CONGRESS.

A complete History of Chess in America and Europe, with Morphy's best games. By D. W. Fiske, editor of *Chess Monthly* (assisted by Morphy and Paulsen). Price $1 50.

BEATRICE CENCI.

A Historical Novel. By F. D. Guerrazzi. Translated from the original Italian by Luigi Monti. Muslin, two volumes in one, with steel portrait, price $1 25.

ISABELLA ORSINI.

A new historical novel. By F. D. Guerrazzi, author of "Beatrice Cenci." Translated by Monti, of Harvard College. With steel portrait. Muslin, price $1 25.

WOMAN'S THOUGHTS ABOUT WOMEN.

The latest and best work by the author of "John Halifax, Gentleman," "Agatha's Husband," "The Ogilvies," &c. From the London edition. Muslin, price $1 00.

AFTERNOON OF UNMARRIED LIFE.

An interesting them admirably treated. Companion to Miss Maloch's "Woman's Thoughts about Women." From London edition. 12mo., muslin, price $1 00.

THE CULPRIT FAY.

By JOSEPH RODMAN DRAKE. A charming edition of this world-celebrated Faery Poem. Printed on colored paper. 12mo., muslin, with frontispiece. Price 50 cts.

THE HABITS OF GOOD SOCIETY.

A valuable handbook for Ladies and Gentlemen; with thoughts, hints, and anecdotes, concerning social observances, taste, and good manners. Muslin, price $1 25.

LECTURES OF LOLA MONTEZ.

Including her "Autobiography," "Wits and Women of Paris," "Comic Aspect of Love," "Gallantry," &c. A new edition, large 12mo., muslin, price $1 25.

CURIOSITIES OF NATURAL HISTORY.

By FRANCIS T. BUCKLAND. Interesting and instructive illustrations and sketches in Natural History. From the London edition. One vol., muslin, price $1 25.

VERNON GROVE;

By Mrs. CAROLINE H. GLOVER. "A Novel which will give its author high rank among the novelists of the day."—*Atlantic Monthly.* 12mo., muslin, price $1 00.

MOTHER GOOSE FOR GROWN FOLKS.

Humorous rhymes based upon the famous "Mother Goose Nursery Melodies." Attractively printed on tinted paper, with frontispiece. Muslin price, 75 cts.

EDGAR POE AND HIS CRITICS.

By Mrs. SARAH H. WHITMAN. Embracing a sketch of the life, and many incidents in the history and family of Edgar Allan Poe. 12mo., muslin. Price 75 cents.

www.ingramcontent.com/pod-product-compliance
Lightning Source LLC
Chambersburg PA
CBHW022022080426
42733CB00007B/686